# Life By Rhyme

Sammy Maddra

Life By Rhyme  © 2022 Sammy Maddra

All rights reserved.



Sammy Maddra asserts the moral right to be identified as author of this work.

Presentation by *BookLeaf Publishing*

Web: www.bookleafpub.com

E-mail: info@bookleafpub.com

ISBN: 9789357616683

First edition 2022

# ACKNOWLEDGEMENT

Thank you to everyone who has taken the time to read my poems and share comments of enthusiasm and encouragement.

# PREFACE

I have been a lover of poetry and rhyme since a young age. When the opportunity arose for me to write and share some poems, I was delighted to take the challenge. I hope you enjoy reading these poems as much as I have enjoyed writing them.

# Innocence and Imagination

Once upon a time
In every child's life
There is a place for innocence
Free from trouble and strife

When Easter bunnies come
With sweet chocolate eggs
And grandma creates toys
In the form of dolly pegs

With summer nights staying up late
And long school season holiday
Made for quests and adventures
With fears and worries faraway

When witches and ghouls
Are something to fear
And Halloween in fall
Is the scariest time of year

Sparklers on bonfire night
Create a majestic atmosphere
With guy Fawkes in a wheelbarrow
And toffee apples around a bonfire

Christmas is full of magic
With presents under the tree
Scents of gingerbread fill the air
With letters to Santa up the chimney

Sleds in the fallen snow
With woolly hats a plenty
Decorating chestnuts
And spending a penny

Mittens on little hands
Scarfs hold off the cold
New Year full of promises
As we quickly grow old

# Just for one day

Slow down just for one day,
Please let the waters be calmed.
Let me catch my breath today,
Please don't let me be alarmed.

Let the tide of emotions rest,
Allow them all to be at peace.
Just for one day, let the birds settle,
And the clouds in the sky decrease.

Let the cherubs be safe today,
To be content and nourished.
Show them that the world is pleasant,
Let them feel they're cherished.

Let the skies of many be bright,
Brighter than all their darkness
And even if it's dark sometimes
The stars remind them of endurance.

And if it can so be today,
Let them only see the good.
Just for one single day,
Let the world be full of love.

# Mind Ache

The trap of the mind
A hunters caged prey

Stuck in a wasp's nest
Like a needle in hay

Drowning in the sea
Sinking in the sand

Chaotic racing motors
Zig zagging through land

A constant chatter
Exacerbating head ache

Looking for fish
In a murky lake

Stuck on a treadmill
Going too fast

Running a race
Always coming last

Butterfly's parade

For no reason

The heart quickens
During social season

Everything's grey
Even the sun

A flower once pretty
Lifeless and glum

The fallen leafs
Lost their magic

A beautiful candle
Made without a wick

Words get stuck
Upon ones chest

Silence the noise
Give it a rest

# The Small Stuff

Sour milk in your morning brew
Chewing gum stuck on your shoe
A traffic jam on your morning commute
A healthy bowl of rotting fruit

Oh the despair

Finding a hair in your gourmet dinner
Looking in the mirror; wishing to be thinner
Washing your hair and it starting to rain
Having Prosecco instead of champagne

Oh the despair

A Red wine stain on a crisp white shirt
Stubbing your toe; oh how it hurts
Standing on Lego a crippling pain
Breaking a clasp on a necklace chain

Oh the despair

A hole in your sock, ladders in tights
Something red in a wash load of whites
A soggy sandwich at lunch break
Trying to sleep but staying awake

Oh the despair

Traffic moving slow; missing a green light
An unexpected bill when money is tight
Nowhere to park when you're running late
An undercooked chip on your dinner plate

Oh the despair

A scuffed wheel trim from hitting the curb
Forgetting to set the phone on 'do not disturb'
Feeling your sock is a little bit damp
The bulb going out on your night lamp

Oh the despair

Passive remarks from someone you love
Losing one of your favourite gloves
A damp sleeve from washing the pots
Combing your hair when it's full of knots

Oh the despair

Although at times the journey feels rough
Remember not to sweat the small stuff

# Autumn: A time to let go

Green gives way to yellow, orange and gold,
The evening sun fades, accepting the dark.
Just before winter does take bitter hold,
Begins fading the sweet song of the lark.

Horse nuts fall upon a leafy wet floor;
A dewy rug so abundantly brown.
Embers burn brightly in the night a-glare,
Petals drop being released from their crown.

Soft winds blow full of a refreshing grace,
Pumpkins galore sit in decoration.
Air so crisp upon the cheeks of a face,
Woodland wildlife begins hibernation.

It is nature's message once every year,
A gentle reminder; let go my dear.

# Within these walls

Four white-washed walls of safety.
A clinicians vault of trust within,
Faith built on deep understanding,
A truth seeking journey they begin.

A mind to guide a broken mind,
From intrenched darkness to light.
Weaving around a broken cortex,
Directing blindness toward insight.

Traumas path; an unhealthy pilgrimage
Has distorted one's very essence
As a world of dark secrets unravels,
From infancy, through to adolescence.

Memories course through life's troubles,
Creating cracks upon the surface scars,
A face of care to greet the misunderstood,
The passage is not but 1; it is but ours.

With those dependable walls of safety,
Inside the cavern of unbroken trust,
The broken layers of trauma's victim.
Are dissected down to specs of dust.

To hold the space, to heal old wounds,
To sit with those in grief and despair.
To mend a mind is to mend a heart,
A personal quality, so uniquely rare.

# Oh, what joy

Oh, what joy
it does bring,
In the form
of a little thing.
Colours dancing
on the wall,
Chasing shadows
after night fall.
A production of flickers
and merry swirls,
The light and dark
embrace in twirls.
Its gentle offering
dim in a room,
Bright on its own,
forces out gloom.
It's calming presence
of a peaceful state,
A romantic gesture
on a first date.
Oh the joy
of simple things,
A wax candle
and the love it brings.

# The Magic of Life

The magic of life

If there is nothing more,
After this life but death,
Why so much detail in leaf?
Why the magic in its breath?
Why the power of a waterfall,
crashing down upon the earth?
Why the beauty of a woman?
and her gift of life and birth?
Why do we gaze into loving eyes?
and wonder through to their soul?
Why the almighty vast emotions?
Why do we oblige to growing old?
Why the intensity of hands interlocking;
fitting together as perfect as can be?
Why the eternal strength of connection?
Between our favourite you and me?
Why the difference in all creatures,
Upon the Earth looking to thrive?
Why do we recognise their character?
With whom we share a desire to survive?
Why the poetic beautiful Sun set?
Or the colours of Autumn in fall?
Why the enchanting stars at night?

Or the hooting of an owl's late call?
Why the waves upon the ocean?
Why the buzzing of a bumblebee?
Why the need for tiny wings on a fly?
Why the defined bark on a tree?
Why do we long for lasting love?
Why do we need to be fulfilled?
Why, if this is all there is to be,
Why is it that death is unwilled?

# Tree

How grand it is; your stature
the shadow you cast on the ground
Almighty, it is how you stand there
So tall and proud and grand

Who knows all that you've seen
The years, the centuries passed by
No-one knows the depth of knowledge
You have kept stored deep inside

How many nests have you homed?
Too many to possibly keep count
How many storms have you weathered
How many wars can you account?

The life you have given so freely
To every life upon this earth
Should be appreciated by masses
And be testament to your worth

# Mans fur friend

Two big shiny chestnut eyes
Full of love and adoration
A pure and innocent soul
The maker's most loyal creation

Four legs made for bouncing
And running amok
Through fields and meadows,
Rolling around in muck

A wagging tail of excitement
That spins around in glee
A sign of complete happiness
On display for all to see

A wet nose full of wonder
That can sniff out anything
The scents that take a fancy
Are almost everything

Joy found in simple delights,
A toy, a sock, a treat, a walk,
Time spent sat listening
To your favourite human talk

A guard of safe protection
To shield those loved most
A bark so loud and warning,
Sometimes used just to boast

Perfectly formed paw prints
That leads the way along
Leaving marks of true devotion
That remains long after you're gone

# Essence

Essence

The crucial things we cannot see or touch
Instead, we use words rich with meaning
In an attempt to capture our essence,
And describe a deeply provoked feeling

Woven within all our good deeds done
Rooted within all our decisions made
Enriching the friendships we create
Defining what it means to be afraid

Deciding our fate and road ahead,
Sculpturing the lover we have chosen
Depicting the enemies we make
Punishment for the rules we've broken

Love and joy, excitement and trust;
Sadness and grief, anger and strife
We cannot hear them or taste them
Yet they consume all the days of our life

# Cover Me

Cover me

Cover me in kisses,
And cuddles too,
Shower me with dreams,
That belong to only you.

Cover me with affection.
Like all things anew,
Draw me in tightly.
Until I breathe only you.

Cover me in truths,
Your heart preciously holds,
Tell me your secrets,
Before the night folds.

Cover me in intimacy,
Only you and I know,
Take me to places,
You know how to go.

Cover me with lies.
The ones I need to hear,
Spare me the truth,

And the pain, my dear.

Cover me in silence,
Keep your anger at bay,
Let's not argue,
When there's so little to say.

Cover me in years,
Of timeless devotion,
Let me wrap you up,
As the one I've chosen.

# Adoration

Oh, how I do adore thee
More than ye shall ever know
More than the stars, the sun and moon
More than summer meadows full in bloom

Oh, how my love does make me feel absurd
For how is it I understand your every word?
You are more than my very own life's worth
More than the pastures of nature's earth

Why must I love thee all so abundantly?
Why does love have to feel so clumsy?

# 2 Syllable's

A simple thing
A five letter word
Can move mountains
When rightful heard

It blesses the ears
And soothes the heart
Spoken in truth
Mends a ruptured depart

It holds the power
To end a bitter war
To call it a truce
To even the score

It justifies a reaction
Validates one reality
Stops those in disagree
And empowers the guilty

A word for the brave at heart
A concise word to end a plight
Two syllables is all it takes
To apologise and stop a fight

# Choose joy

Life is too abundantly full
Of trials and tribulations
Too short to sit and dwell
In all its difficult situations

If every obstacle you encounter
Gets and exasperated response
Then life will feel too heavy
It's better to be nonchalance

For if every unmet expectation
Proceeded with a level of defeat
Remember to give more, take less
And know you are already complete

When looking at a grey sky,
Dwell upon the rain's vitality
And how it nourishes the land
Simply change your mentality

With a world getting high on stress
And pressure becoming superior
Stop and pause for a moment
Look around at the miracle of nature

Within a clear mind and heart
Know that it can always be seen
Choose joy in the form of little things
The highs, the lows and the in between

# Sunset

The line of the ocean meeting the sky
Just at the start of night fall
Like peacefully tucking the world away
Designed to dramatically enthral

The colours are majestic on display
Like the colours of the rainbow
Pacing themselves 1, 2 at a time
As the sun moves down slow

Taking its time to dip in the sea
Carefully, decidedly not too quick
To be sure, the show is perfect
The movement is completely slick

The awe inspiration of the night sky
Can be enjoyed whilst on the beach
Caressing every human eye
A sunset; no man can reach

# Hormones

25

Hormones, hormones everywhere!
And not one HRT patch to spare!

There's hot flushes, a many
Anxiety is through the roof
Tempers gone from 0 to 100
She's feeling pretty aloof

Breasts a bulging
Joints are aching
All in the name
Of goddamn ageing

Her mind is at a stand still
They call it brain fog
Might as well detach her head
And flush it down the bog

Wrinkles appearing here and there
Or so she frequently says
Despite a tub of 50 pound cream
Applied a million times a day

Convinced that her bottom
Has grown overnight

Although her everyday clothes
Are not even close to tight

"Sleep" I hear her say
"Now what the hell is that,"
There's no such thing for a woman
Who's new regime is like a bat

Vitamins and supplements
Replace vodka and take always
In a bid, to manage the symptoms
She's even started to pray

So tell me Mother Nature
Why oh why punish us women?
After years of hard labour
Must we have this absurd disposition?

# In the end

If you were gone today,
Not to the shop or on vacation,
But truly gone for good,
Would you of had a positive persuasion?

In the end, would you be pleased?
Would your heart be satisfied?
Not by the way you dressed,
Or how you decorated your eyes.

In the end, would it really matter?
Would anyone of given thought?
Of your hair or nail colour?
Or the brand of clothes you bought?

In the end, would anyone care,
If you drove a convertible or a hatchback?
What matters most is the miles in your heart,
And the love that you freely gave back.

In the end were you a gossip?
Or could you hold the privacy of another?
We're you as loyal as a lion?
Or did you speak the secrets of others?

In the end, could you recognise,
The suffering felt by other people?
Could you hold space to help them?
Or did you turn a blind eye to evil?

In the end, did you remain faithful?
To your partner, child and friend?
Did you pave a way for support?
On you, could they depend?

In the end, did you speak the truth?
With virtue, peace, and care?
Did you respect the rights of others?
And their right to be treated fair?

In the end, we're you true to yourself?
Did you walk the words you spoke?
Or were you a hypocrite in disguise?
Did you hide behind a fake cloak?

In the end, what matters most,
When laying your head to rest.
Knowing no matter what happens,
You did your very best!

# How do we measure a life?

Is it the cups of smiles shared,
Or the miles of distance travelled?
Is it the kilograms of joy in a day,
Or the amount of lies unravelled?

Is it the kindness we measure,
Not by length, but depth instead?
Or Is it the money we gather,
Or how fast we run to get ahead?

Is it the figure of deeds done for others,
Or is it personal growth and prosperity?
Is it the count of a life's worth of lovers,
Or the endurance in a careers longevity?

Is it the sum total of charity given?
Or is it the decimal point of fortune?
Is it the collection of medals on a wall,
Or a total of triumphs after misfortune?

Can we measure the acts of integrity,
Or the truth in prayers sent up above?
Is it ounces of compassion given freely,
Or the beats in a heart that spreads love?

# Have you ever

Have you ever watched light fade from
someone's eyes?
A distressing moment just before a person dies.
The final breath surrendering at the end,
Right before you feel their soul ascend.
Have you ever held a precious hand so tight?
Just like you and death are in a direct fight.
The moment you feel them loosen their grasp,
Without any rehearsals, the moment has passed.
Have you ever observed clothes hanging on a
rail?
Once full of life, now empty and frail,
A watch without a wrist, rings without fingers,
Upon on old pillow, their scent still lingers.
Have you ever prayed to a God you don't believe
in?
And every other God that there has ever been.
Have you made a wish to the heavens above,
To spare the life of someone you love?
Have you ever cried from the depths of despair?
Feeling trapped, suffocated, and robbed of air.
Broken inside, helpless and lost,
Wanting them back, whatever the cost.
Have you ever missed a smile, a laugh, and a
cry?

Knowing that forever was key in your last
goodbye.
You will never hear their voice or feel their
touch,
All you're left with is missing them too much.
Have you ever experienced a broken heart?
And felt your soul being torn apart.

Have you ever lost someone you can't live
without?

# Look for me

Look for me in sun rays,
casting light from way up high.
Look for me in moon beams,
and stars across the night sky.

Look for me in fallen leaves,
upon the autumn ground.
Look for me in the morning birds,
and the sweetness of their sound.

Look for me on raindrops,
falling hard upon your face.
Look for me in snowflakes,
falling gently, full of grace.

Look for me in springs fresh flowers,
depicting new beginnings.
Look for me in celebrations,
decorations, bunting and the trimmings.

Look for me in music,
hear me in every note.
Look for me in the stories,
my life so preciously wrote.

Look for me in your laughter,
And in your tears too.
Look for me in times of sadness,
I'll still bring comfort to you.

Look for me in your memories,
and you will see I still go on.
Look for me in the things around you,
And I will never be truly gone.

www.ingramcontent.com/pod-product-compliance
Lightning Source LLC
LaVergne TN
LVHW010928200726

843509LV00013B/2128